The World of Work

Rhoda McFarland

THE ROSEN PUBLISHING GROUP, INC.
NEW YORK

Published in 1993 by The Rosen Publishing Group, Inc.
29 East 21st Street, New York, NY 10010

First Edition
Copyright 1993 by The Rosen Publishing Group, Inc.

All rights reserved. No part of this book may be reproduced in any form without permission in writing from the publisher, except by a reviewer.

Manufactured in the United States of America

Library of Congress Cataloging-in-Publication Data
McFarland, Rhoda.
    The world of work/ by Rhoda McFarland
    (The Life skills library)
    Includes bibliographical references and index.
    Summary: Presents information on job hunting, appearance, interviews, defining work objectives, salary, tips, résumés, scheduling, and planning ahead.
    ISBN 0-8239-1467-4
    1. Job hunting—Juvenile literature. 2. Employment Interviewing—Juvenile literature. [1. Job hunting. 2. Employment Interviewing. 3. Vocational Guidance.] I. Title II. Series.
HF5382.7.M395 1992
650.14—dc20
                                                        92-11044
                                                             CIP
                                                              AC

CONTENTS

Chapter 1	So You Want to Get a Job	5
Chapter 2	Before You Look for a Job	9
Chapter 3	Preparing for the Job Hunt	15
Chapter 4	Applying for the Job	21
Chapter 5	The Job Interview	26
Chapter 6	Being a Good Employee	30
Chapter 7	Managing Your Money	35
Chapter 8	Managing Your Time	38
Chapter 9	Looking to the Future	41
	Glossary—Explaining New Words	45
	For Further Reading	46
	Index	47

SO YOU WANT TO GET A JOB

"**I** hate to ask for money," Jenny grumbled. "I have to find a job." It was lunchtime. Jenny and her friends were talking about the trip to Disney World MGM during spring break.

"I know my parents can't give me the money for the trip," Mark said. "They're getting me a car for my birthday next month. I'm going to have to get a job, too. If I want the car I have to pay for insurance and gas. And I need money for a lot of other things. I know what you mean about asking. I'd rather have a job of my own."

"There aren't many jobs, and a lot of kids are looking for work," Mike said. "It's easy to say you'll get a job. It's a lot harder to get one."

Part-time jobs teach you about work-related responsibilities.

THE WORLD OF WORK

"Burger Barn has a help-wanted sign up," Amy offered.

"Penny asked about that," Jon put in. "They want someone from 6 p.m. to 10 p.m. I know I'd have a hard time getting my homework done. Besides, I wouldn't want to work fast food."

"Right now, I'm not particular," Jenny said. "I may go down and see about that. What's the big deal about handing hamburgers to people?"

"I'm with Jon. I don't want to work fast food," Mark said. "I haven't really needed a job until now, but I guess I'd better start getting serious about it."

"One thing's for sure, Jenny, you'll never make any money working at Burger Barn. They only pay minimum wage," Mike told her.

"I don't care what it pays," Jon said. "I wouldn't work at the Burger Barn. I hate being inside all the time. I don't want to sweep floors either."

"What do you *want* to do?" asked Mike.

"I'm not sure, but I know what I don't want to do."

"I don't know what I *can* do," Amy said. "It's hard to get a job without experience, and it's hard to get experience if you can't get a job."

"Yeah, how can you get a job when nobody will hire you without experience?" Terry wanted to know.

"Stacey had to take a typing test to get her job. They wanted someone who could type 50 words a minute. She didn't have to have experience," Jenny told them.

So You Want to Get a Job

"Well, I can't type 50 words a minute, so I'd never be able to pass a typing test." Amy looked so sad that everyone laughed.

"Don't worry, Amy, there are lots of jobs where you don't have to pass a typing test," Mark teased. "Your brother didn't have to type to be a lifeguard last summer."

"He had to pass a lifesaving test, and I can't do that either. You just make me feel worse, Mark."

A Job Is a Business Deal

Going to work is a business deal between you and your employer. You sell your skills and your time. Your employer buys those skills and that time, and pays you money for them. Stacey sells her skill as a typist. Her work time is worth more than Amy's because Amy has no special skill or training. How much you are paid for your working time depends on the skills and abilities you have to sell.

Since Amy and Jenny have no training or special skills, they are said to be unskilled. Your time and effort are your only resources if you are unskilled. For most high-school students, only unskilled jobs are available.

Besides the low pay, unskilled jobs offer few chances to advance. The skills you learn do not prepare you for a better job.

You can raise your value to an employer if you improve your skills or learn new ones. You can do that in some businesses while you work. Some

employers offer on-the-job training for employees. You learn a skill from an experienced worker during the workday. High schools often have work experience programs that give you on-the-job training. You can prepare yourself by taking classes to learn a skill, as Stacey did. Community colleges have programs that prepare you for a variety of jobs. There are vocational schools that teach skills. High schools, community colleges, and universities offer night classes. These are just a few of the ways to raise your value to an employer.

Making Job Choices

For right now, you may be satisfied with an unskilled job. Jenny wants money for the extra things her parents can't afford to give her. She is willing to work anywhere for any pay. Stacey took typing and other business courses because she wants to work in an office. Mike isn't sure what he wants to do.

Jenny knows why she wants to work. Stacey knows where she wants to work. To Jon, doing well in school is more important than a job right now. Mark seems to be looking for a job that pays well.

People have many reasons for choosing jobs. You need to know what skills you have to sell to an employer. You need to explore your abilities and interests, your likes and dislikes. You need to know how to present yourself to an employer on paper and in person. Being prepared can open the door to the interesting world of work.

CHAPTER 2

BEFORE YOU LOOK FOR A JOB

Chewing the end of her pen, Amy was deep in thought. Mike saw her when he went into the library. "What are you working on, Amy?" he asked.

"Oh, hi, Mike. These are forms that Ms. Hanson at the career center gave me. They're supposed to help me find out what my interests and abilities are. Ms. Hanson says I need to know my strengths and weaknesses so I can get a job that's right for me. She says I'll learn what personal skills I have that are important to employers," Amy explained.

"What's this under Strengths and Weaknesses—physical characteristics, aptitudes, and personality traits?" Mike asked as he looked at the papers.

"Ms. Hanson says these are the three areas we need to look at. For physical characteristics, my

strengths are that I'm very healthy and I'm well coordinated and good in sports. A weakness is that I'm only 5 feet tall and weigh 101 pounds. I'm just not strong enough for some jobs."

"So an aptitude might be that I'm good in math," Mike said. "And a weakness would be that I'm a terrible speller."

"That's right," Amy agreed. "An aptitude of mine is that I'm a good singer. A weakness is that I don't write very well."

"A personality strength is something like being on time or being cheerful, right?" Mike said. "This shouldn't be too hard to fill out."

"It's sure making me think," Amy told him.

Mike picked up two other papers that Amy had. "What are these? You did them already."

"Those are for interests and abilities," Amy explained. "You put all of these together, and you find out all about yourself."

"Do you think if I do this I'll be able to figure out what kind of job I want?" Mike asked.

"It should help anyway," was Amy's answer.

Get to Know Yourself

Amy and Mike, like you, have qualities that are valuable in the job market. Also like them, you may not be aware of what you have to offer. It's time to get to know yourself.

Reading through the help-wanted ads in your local newspaper is a good way to start your job search.

THE WORLD OF WORK

Know Your Aptitudes

Aptitudes are abilities and talents. They may be developed or undeveloped. You may have an aptitude for fixing mechanical things. However, you won't be able to fix a car until you develop your ability to do that.

A talent for drawing is easy to see at an early age. The ability to deal with people is harder to find out about. Sometimes more than one ability is needed to do a job. To be a successful employee in a beauty salon you must have the knowledge and skills for styling hair. In addition, you must be able to work well with people. Use the following list to help you identify some of your aptitudes.

___ running	___ talking to people	___ cooking
___ math	___ listening to people	___ typing
___ reading	___ using a calculator	___ acting
___ selling	___ using common sense	___ helping
___ writing	___ working in a group	___ organizing
___ drawing	___ repairing things	___ solving problems
___ singing	___ using my hands	___ gardening
___ remembering	___ playing an instrument	___ sports
___ construction	___ telling stories	___ leading a group
___ child care	___ animal care	___ fixing things
___ sewing	___ drawing cartoons	___ things not on list

By discovering your aptitudes, you can try things out. If you never discover your aptitudes, you may miss out on something you could be interested in.

Know Your Interests

You may do some things well that you don't like to do. You may be very good at sweeping the floor. That doesn't mean you are interested in doing that.

Knowing your interests may lead you to discover abilities you never knew you had. Mike likes to build things. He took wood shop this year. He is building a table and chairs for the dining room at home. He didn't know that he would have to draw his own plans before he could make the dining set. Now Mike is so good at drawing plans that other students come to him for help. Mike's interest in building led him to discover his drawing ability.

Look at the aptitude list again. Check those items that are interests as well as aptitudes. Then make your own list of interests. Be sure to include activities you like to do, such as biking, fishing, skiing, swimming, diving, listening to music, driving a car, skateboarding, being with friends, or collecting baseball cards.

Know Your Personality Traits

Besides interests and abilities, you have characteristics that make you different from everyone else. Those traits make you more suited for some jobs than for others. If you are very shy, working as a host in a restaurant is probably not for you.

Look at the following list of personality traits. Check the ones that describe you.

___friendly	___affectionate	___kind	___strong
___cheerful	___flexible	___on time	___capable
___trusting	___cooperative	___thinker	___caring
___confident	___careful	___steady	___leader
___fair	___outgoing	___honest	___neat
___positive	___interested	___faithful	___shy
___ambitious	___respectful	___loyal	___helpful
___easygoing	___understanding	___quiet	___certain
___independent	___dependable	___active	___gentle

Know Your Strengths and Weaknesses

Using your lists of personality traits, abilities, and physical characteristics, make a list of your strengths and weaknesses.

Look again at your list of interests. Do any of your interests fit your strengths? Amy has a way with animals. Her interest in animals is matched by her ability to handle them. Mike is the fastest runner in his gym class, but he has no interest in being on the track team. It's possible that the things you do well may not always be the things you like to do. Try to match your interests with your strengths.

Know Your Physical Self

You have physical strengths and weaknesses. A bad knee keeps you from doing work that would stress the knee. Upper-body strength makes it possible to lift and carry. Make a list of your physical characteristics. What might limit your physical activities? What will help you do the job?

CHAPTER 3

PREPARING FOR THE JOB HUNT

Looking very upset when she joined the group, Jenny sat next to Mark. "You don't look very happy, Jen. What's the matter?"

"I'm mad. I just found out that I have to have a social security number before I can even apply for a job. I talked to Ms. Hanson. She told me about the social security number and gave me an application for one. There's no office here, so I have to mail it. It will take at least two weeks, maybe more, before I get a card with the number. Meanwhile, I can't get a job," Jenny moaned.

"You can get all the other stuff done while you wait," Amy reminded Jenny. "I'm working on my résumé. Ms. Hanson said she'd help me, but I have to at least write the first draft myself."

"She said something about a cover letter, too, whatever that is," Mike put in. "You can't expect to find a job the first day you look for one either. You have to look around a while. There's lots to do while you wait for your social security card."

Your Social Security Number

Every worker must have a social security number and card. Your employer must report your income to the government, using your social security number to identify you. You then pay taxes on all wages reported to the government. Your number is on your social security account. You may receive income from your account when you retire. If you are not able to work, you may also receive special payments from social security.

Today, parents must give a social security number for each child they claim on their federal income tax. You probably already have a number.

If you do not have a social security card, apply for one as soon as possible. The career counselor or guidance office in your school may have applications. Some public libraries, post offices, and banks have them, too.

You must show proof of your identity, age, and U.S. citizenship when you apply. A birth certificate or baptismal certificate proves your age and citizenship. Copies of certificates are not accepted.

Odd jobs for neighbors count as good work experience.

A driver's license or a school ID card or report card will prove your identity. Any document that has a physical description, photograph, or signature is acceptable. All documents will be returned to you.

If you are 18 or older and have never had a social security number, you must apply *in person* at a social security office. Also if you are *not* a U.S. citizen, you must apply in person.

Your Résumé

A résumé is a one-page summary of facts about you. It tells an employer what knowledge, interests, skills, and personal qualities you will bring to a job. A résumé usually includes five sections:

Personal Information
- Your full name (first, middle initial, last)
- Your address (street number, street name, apartment number, city, state, ZIP code)
- Your phone number (including area code)

Education History
- High school (name of the last high school you attended, city, and dates you went there)
- Any training or vocational courses

Work Experience
- List any jobs you have had, starting with the most recent one. Give the dates you worked there and your employer's name and address.

- If you have not had formal work experience, list any jobs you have done, including mowing lawns, delivering papers, helping to maintain family cars, baby-sitting, cooking, or cleaning house.

Special Interests and Skills
- List your hobbies, school activities, community activities, and clubs.
- List any skills you have. Include such things as "Work well with young children" if you baby-sit, "Know how to use power tools" if you took shop in school or work at home, "Mechanical ability" if you are good at fixing things.
- List any honors or awards you've won.

References
- List the names, addresses, and phone numbers of three people who know you well. Be sure to ask people before you use them as references and write a thank-you note to each one. You might ask teachers, ministers, adult friends, or school counselors.

Writing Your Résumé

Your lists of abilities, interests, and strengths will help you write your résumé. You may find it hard at first. Use Amy's résumé to help you with yours.

The résumé should be typed or printed, with no errors or misspelled words. Make several copies of your résumé. You will be able to use it for more than one employer.

Résumé

Amy L. Collins
2265 Ocean Avenue
Palm Bay, FL 32905
Telephone (407) 555-8899

Education

September, 1990-Present Malibar High School, Palm Bay, Florida. I will graduate in June 1994.

Work Experience

Summers, 1990, 1991 Cared for 3 children ages 4, 6, and 9 Monday-Friday from 7:30 a.m. to 5:30 p.m. Cared for them two evenings a week during the school year. Also cooked meals and cleaned house.

September, 1990-June, 1991 Secretary's assistant in school office. Duties: answered telephone and took messages, used copy machine, filed, used intercom, sorted mail.

Special Interests and Skills

Activities - volleyball, Camera Club, choir at school and at church

Interests - enjoy animals, music, dancing, swimming, bicycling, photography

Skills - work well with young children; bathe and groom dogs; can answer and direct calls on a six-line telephone, run a copy machine—including sorting and reducing and enlarging copies—do alphabetical filing; use an intercom system; able to follow directions and complete a job

Awards - Perfect Attendance Award in 1989 and 1991

References

Ruth Edwards
456 Whistler Drive
Palm Bay, FL 32905
(407) 555-2345

Jean Miller, Secretary
Malibar High School
1789 Weston Road
Palm Bay, FL 32905
(407) 555-5321

Richard Williams
Advisor, Camera Club
Malibar High School
1789 Weston Road
Palm Bay, FL 32905
(407) 555-5321

APPLYING FOR THE JOB

"Hey, Amy, wait up!" Mike shouted. "I've been looking all over for you," he said when he caught up with her.

"What's the big deal?" Amy wanted to know.

"I found out about a job you might like," Mike said. He sounded excited.

"Great," Amy answered. "Tell me about it."

"It's with Bill Norris, a friend of my father. He's looking for someone to answer the phone and take messages in his office. It would be from 4 p.m. to 6 p.m. during the week and 10 a.m. to 6 p.m. on Saturday."

"What do I have to do to find out more about it?" Amy asked Mike.

"Mr. Norris said mail your résumé to his office. He'll get in touch with you if he's interested. I here the bell, I'll give you the address at lunch time."

When they all met later in the cafeteria, Amy asked Mike about the office job. Then she asked how his job search was going.

"I've been watching the ads in the paper," Mike said. "Ms. Hanson said she'll let me know about any jobs that come into her office.

"Since we did our interests and abilities and all, I found out I can do a lot more than I thought. I really like woodworking. Ms. Hanson thinks I can get a job with a cabinetmaker. I'm thinking about maybe trying to find a landscaping company that will hire me. I'd like to learn how to design landscaping for homes or office buildings. I didn't even think of mowing lawns as experience until I made my résumé."

"How do you find a company to work for if Ms. Hanson doesn't hear from any?" Mark wanted to know.

"My dad says the Yellow Pages are a good place to find companies you might want to work for," Amy told him. "He said to call the personnel office and ask if they have any jobs."

"My brother went to the State Employment Office. They have a big list of jobs," Jenny said.

Your Job Search

Knowing *where* to look for a job is very important. By working with Ms. Hanson, Mike is using one of

A hobby or special interest can become a marketable job skill.

The World of Work

the most important resources he has. Your school career counselors or teachers who are in charge of the outside work program are a good place to start. Employers often list job openings with schools.

Newspaper classified ads, often called want ads, are lists of job openings. Government jobs are often posted on bulletin boards in post offices, city and county office buildings, and state employment offices. Sometimes cities, counties, and states have special youth employment services. Some churches and business organizations support job placement services for youth.

Mike went to a union hall to see about a job with a cabinetmaker. The union hall is the headquarters for a labor union. Carpenters, plumbers, and electricians are some of the trades that have unions. The unions often do the hiring for the companies in the area.

Some jobs are listed with employment agencies. The agency charges a fee. Sometimes the employer pays the fee. Other times the applicant pays it. If you use an agency, be sure you know who pays the fee.

The Yellow Pages of the telephone book can give you ideas of businesses to contact. You can call and ask for the personnel office.

Walk around town and the shopping malls. See if there are any "Help Wanted" signs in windows.

Many times friends or relatives know about jobs. Also they will tell their friends about you. Neighbors, teachers, and ministers are good sources of job information, too.

The Cover Letter

When a résumé is mailed, a cover letter, also called a letter of application, should be sent with it.

A cover letter should be only one typed page. It should have three or four paragraphs:
- An opening paragraph that tells why you are writing.
- A short paragraph that tells more about you and your skills. Stress your education, if you lack work experience.
- A sentence calling attention to your résumé.
- A final paragraph asking for an interview at the convenience of the employer.

Remember when you write your letter, address the letter to a specific person. If possible, address it to the person doing the hiring. Be sure your spelling, punctuation, and grammar are correct. Send the original letter, not a copy.

The Job Application

Many times you can walk into a business and ask for an application. Read the entire form before you start to complete it. Be neat. It is *very* important that you fill out the application carefully and completely. If there is something that does not apply to you, write N/A in the space provided.

An employer judges you by your application. It is your first showing of yourself to the employer. Your application can open or close the door to a new job.

CHAPTER 5

THE JOB INTERVIEW

Amy hung up the phone and immediately dialed Jenny's number. She couldn't wait to tell the good news. When she heard Jenny's voice, Amy almost shouted. "Jen, I'm going to have an interview for the job!"

"All right! When is it?" Jenny wanted to know.

"Tomorrow after school. I've got to practice tonight. Will you come over and help me?"

"Did you say practice? How do you practice for an interview?" Amy explained to Jenny that it really is possible to practice for an interview. She had a booklet that Ms. Hanson had given her.

Jenny came over that night and worked with Amy. Using Amy's résumé, she made up all kinds of questions. She asked about Amy's hobbies and interests.

Looking your best for a job interview can give you confidence, as well as a better chance at being hired.

She asked about her family, about singing with the choirs at school and church. She wanted to know if working after school would conflict with Amy's playing volleyball or baby-sitting. She asked why Amy wanted to work for this company.

Amy gave answers that were more than "yes" or "no." She wanted to give complete answers without talking too much.

Getting Ready for Your Interview

How you dress and present yourself at your interview is very important. If the employer has your résumé and application, study your copy. Be able to answer personal questions quickly and accurately. Employers want to know how you express yourself.

Be sure you know exactly where you are going for your interview. If possible, get the name of the person who will be interviewing you.

Get to your interview at least ten minutes early. Being late will lower your chances of getting the job.

Find out about the company or business. You may be asked why you want to work for the company.

The Interview

When you go to your interview, go alone. Don't chew gum. When you meet your interviewer, smile and greet her or him by name. Shake hands if the interviewer makes the offer. Sit down when the interviewer invites you to.

Try to relax. The employer wants to hire someone, so that is in your favor. But relax doesn't mean slide down and stretch your legs. Your posture tells the interviewer how important you think the job is.

Ask about the job. What is the salary? Are there fringe benefits? What is the work schedule? Will there be a chance of advancement?

Don't boast, but don't put yourself down. Talk about your strengths that would be valuable to the company.

You may be offered a job at the interview. If you are ready to accept the job, do so. If you are not sure this is the job you want, ask for time to think it over. Leave as soon as the interviewer shows the interview is over. Thank her or him for the interview even if you don't think you got the job. Good manners are always in order.

A follow-up letter should be sent immediately. It should be very short and to the point. Thank the person for the interview. State what you want the the interviewer to remember — you liked the job, you are ready to start work immediately. Finally, offer to provide any further information and again thank the interviewer.

BEING A GOOD EMPLOYEE

Their smiles told Ms. Hanson that Penny and Amy had good news. They were both starting work on Monday.

"We just wanted to check with you and see if there's anything else we need to know," Penny said. "We want to get a good start at our jobs."

"Have you thought about what your employer expects of you?" Ms. Hanson asked. "You need to know what employers want most from their employees. You also need to think about what you can expect from your employer."

Ms. Hanson went on to discuss with the girls six characteristics of good employees: regular attendance, loyalty, following instructions, responsibility, good attitude, and willingness to work.

Employers look for people who are friendly and can get along with others.

"That sounds reasonable. I can handle what it takes to be a good employee," Amy stated. "What should we expect from an employer?"

"Employers have responsibilities to you," Ms. Hanson told Amy. "They should teach you how to do your job. You should have a supervisor to look at what you do and tell you how well you're doing."

Then Ms. Hanson talked about some other employer responsibilities. Amy and Penny began to understand that a job is truly a business deal.

Responsibilities of an Employer

Your employer has a responsibility to make it possible for you to do your job safely and well. There are some basic things you can expect from your employer.

Training and supervision. You can't be expected to do your job well unless you are taught how to do it. After you learn your job, you still need a supervisor to see that the work is done right and to answer any questions that you may have.

A clean, safe place to work. State and federal laws require your employer to make your workplace clean and safe. Employers must make you aware of safety rules.

Payment. Wages are paid by the hour. People who are paid a set amount every week or month earn a *salary*.

Fringe benefits. Fringe benefits are something you receive besides your wages or salary. Some employers provide uniforms or free meals. Many companies offer life and health insurance plans. If you are working part time, you may not qualify for fringe benefits.

Fair treatment. Employers should treat all employees equally. When you haven't done your job, you need to be told about it. However, you deserve to be treated respectfully at all times.

Responsibilities of Employees

There are several important things that your employer will expect from you.

Regular attendance. Your time is what you sell to your employer. When you are absent, your work must be done by someone else or go undone.

Loyalty. Being loyal is being faithful. Loyal employees speak well of their employers. They try to do what is best for the company. Employees also need loyalty from one another. Without loyalty, less work usually gets done.

Following instructions. Your supervisor is your team leader. As part of a team, you must follow directions. Employees who do not follow directions are not valuable to an employer.

Responsibility. Being responsible adds to your value as an employee. Being on time and using your time well at work are part of your responsibility.

Employers like employees who can see what has to be done and do it without being told.

Attitude. Your attitude on the job is important. Here are some characteristics of what would be considered a good attitude:

- Being flexible, willing to change
- Being willing to see the other side
- Not making excuses or complaining
- Not being critical of others
- Having a pleasant, friendly manner
- Taking responsibility for your mistakes
- Having respect for others

Willingness to Work. You are of value to your employer only if you do the work you are paid to do. To be valuable as a worker you must develop your skills. You need to practice good work habits. It's important to do your best and work steadily.

CHAPTER 7

MANAGING YOUR MONEY

"Lot of good it does me to work. I never have any money anyway," Mark moaned.

"I thought you were making pretty good money," Jon said.

"I guess I am. But I owed Mom for a pair of sneakers. Last payday I had to pay my car insurance. And I have to put money in savings. I only have $10 to last me until my next payday."

"It sounds like you're spending your money even before you get it," Penny said.

"Mom said something about that when I borrowed the money for my sneakers," Mark said. "She said maybe I should think about budgeting my money and making a purchase after I've saved up for it. Then I wouldn't get caught short so often."

Why Budget?

A budget is a plan for spending money. A budget can help you in several ways:
- It lets you know where your money is going.
- It helps you live on what you make.
- It helps you save for unexpected expenses.
- It helps you plan for buying high-cost items.

Keeping track of your money and your spending helps you get the most out of your paycheck.

Mark's Budget

Mark worked at a grocery store. He was paid $6.50 an hour and worked 18 hours a week. His gross pay before taxes was $234 every two weeks. Federal income tax of $21.34 was taken out. Social security tax was $14.22, and Medicare tax was $3.45. A total of $39.01 was taken out of his check, leaving him with a net income of $194.99.

```
Income: $194.99/every two weeks
Expenses: every two weeks
    Insurance (car)                  50.00
    Transportation (gas, oil)        22.65
    Food (lunch, snacks)             25.00
    Savings                          35.00
    Recreation (movies, tapes,
       bowling, and other)           12.50
    Clothing                         30.00
    Personal                         10.00
    Other                             9.84
                                    194.99

Total Income: $194.99  Total Expenses: $194.99
```

Managing Your Money

There are two kinds of expenses in every budget—necessities and luxuries. Necessities are things that you feel you must have. Luxuries are things you want but can live without.

For his budget, Mark listed necessities first. He had to pay $100 every month for car insurance. He needed $10 a week for gas and $5.30 a month for oil. Lunches were next. He could buy lunch at school for $2 a day. When he went out with friends, Mark liked to have a soda or something. He decided on $10 a month for snacks. That made $40 for lunches and $10 for snacks, or $50 a month for food.

Mark was serious about savings. He wanted to plan for car repairs, senior pictures, and prom and graduation expenses. He decided on $70 a month.

Mark decided that $25 a month for tapes, bowling and other recreation was about right.

Mark had learned from not saving for the sneakers. But he didn't have to buy clothes that often. He thought $60 a month would be enough.

Haircuts were his only personal expense, but just in case something came up, he budgeted $20 for personals.

That left all of $19.68, which he put under "Other" for little unexpected expenses.

Since he was paid every two weeks, Mark decided to make a two-week budget. He divided all of his expenses by 2. Now he knows how much he has to spend each pay period.

Remember, your income must equal your expenses. That is called *balancing* your budget.

CHAPTER 8
MANAGING YOUR TIME

Amy didn't want to see the test that Mr. Reed was handing her. She knew it had an F on it. Since she had started working, she couldn't find enough time to study. Lots of kids worked and still got good grades. Why was she having such a hard time, she wondered?

After class, Amy talked to Penny. "You know my mom helped me make a budget for my money," Penny said. "Well, she helped me make a budget for my time, too."

Penny took a small calendar book out of her bag and showed it to Amy. "I write down the hours I work on my calendar. See, this week I work 5 p.m. to 9 p.m. on Tuesday and Wednesday. I work 4 p.m. to 8 p.m. on Friday, and 10 a.m. to 4 p.m. on Saturday."

A little advance planning can help you make the most of your time.

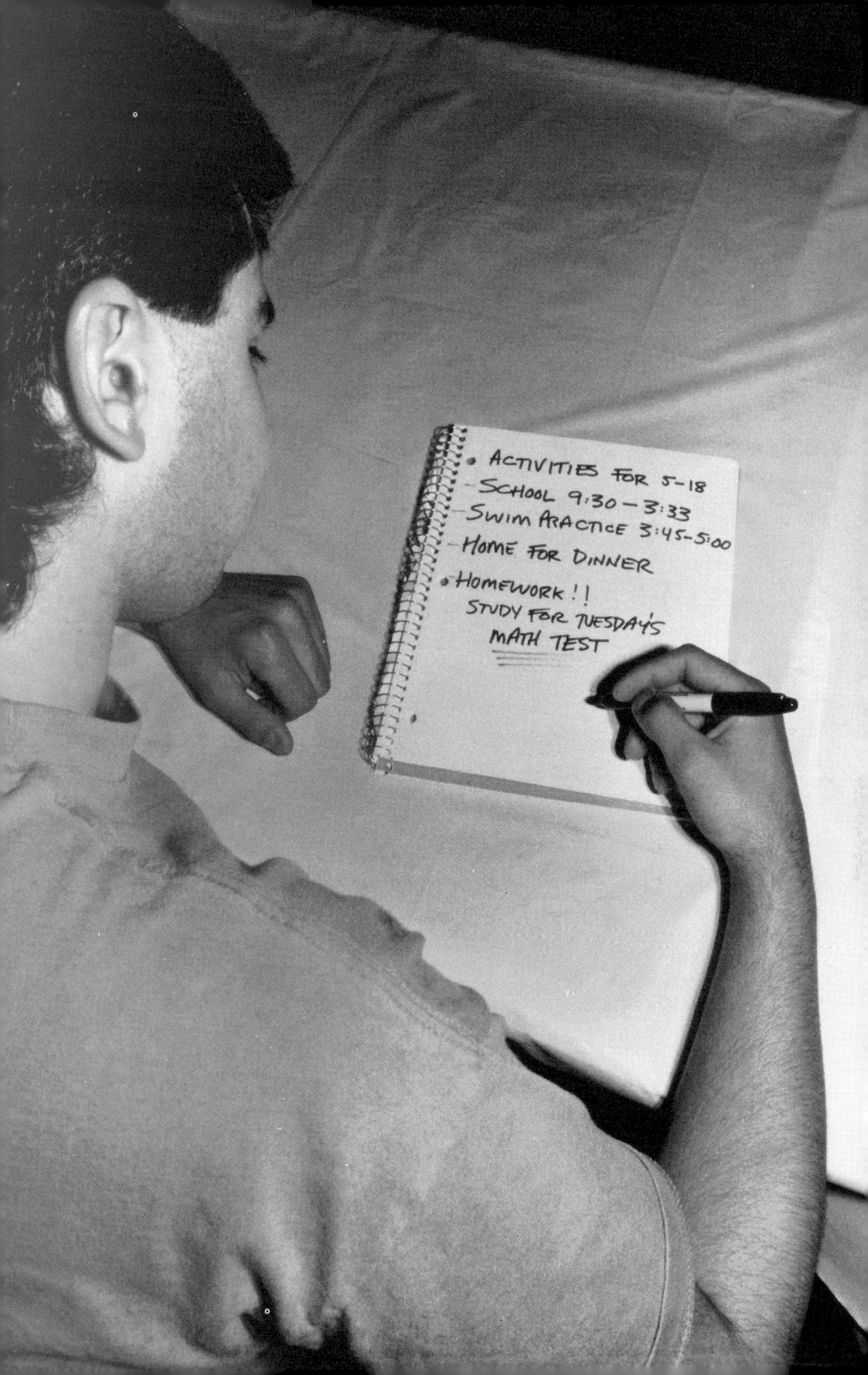

- Activities for 5-18
  - School 9:30 - 3:33
  - Swim Practice 3:45 - 5:00
  - Home for Dinner
- Homework !!
  Study for Tuesday's
  Math Test

Penny told Amy how she scheduled her study time around her work hours. She also planned her fun time, including talking to her friends on the phone. Amy decided a time budget might work for her, too.

Amy works different hours during the week. On a calendar, she marked the days she had to work and the hours involved. She also made notes of any special occasions, such as birthdays and parties. That way, she could arrange with her boss not to be scheduled for work at those times. She used a sheet of lined paper to make her time budget for a regular school day and a work day. She made schedules for Saturday and Sunday, too. Starting with 7 a.m., she listed what she was to do each hour on school days when she had to work and when she had no work, and on Saturdays and Sundays. She marked time for homework, for chores, and for free time.

Making a time budget is simple. Keeping yourself on your budget is the hard part. It is hard to tell your friends that you can only talk on the phone between 9 p.m. and 10 p.m. It isn't easy to go home and study after school when friends are going to hang out until dinner time. Working means more than being responsible at work. It means being responsible about school and spare time as well. It means planning enough time to sleep so you can carry out your responsibilities and enjoy your spare time. Think of your time budget as your key to giving you the most time to enjoy even though you're working and going to school.

CHAPTER 9

LOOKING TO THE FUTURE

For many people, choosing a career is one of the hardest decisions in life. Graduation from high school means taking more responsibility for yourself and making important choices. Many young people don't feel quite ready to take on all the responsibilities and decisions of adulthood. They feel "in between" dependence and independence. To bridge that gap and feel a sense of direction, they need to set career goals.

Finding Job Opportunities

The most complete reference guide for jobs and careers is the *Dictionary of Occupational Titles (DOT)*. The *DOT* is published by the U.S. Department of Labor. It lists more than 20,000 occupations.

Another book put out by the Department of Labor is the *Occupational Outlook Handbook* (*OOH*). The *OOH* is published every year. It lists and describes thousands of jobs. The employment outlook tells which jobs will need workers in the future.

Because the job market changes so quickly, the Bureau of Labor Statistics also publishes the *Occupational Outlook Quarterly* (*OOQ*). Check with your school library or your public library.

Careers and You

If you are not sure what kind of career you want, get help in setting goals and making your career decisions. Your career guidance counselor at school is a good place to start.

Some people have long-range career goals. They know that what they want to do takes years of study and training. Other people have shorter-range goals. As they grow and change they adjust their career goals to fit their needs.

Many people start on one career path and discover it isn't taking them where they want to go. When you start a job, you can't know if you've made a good choice until you work for a while. As you gain experience, you change. As you change, your goals change. You may need higher goals or different goals.

A trained professional in career guidance can help with suggestions about career choices and job opportunities.

You may have life experience that can qualify you to do a job for pay.

Job satisfaction comes to different people for different reasons. Some people like to feel that they are doing something worthwhile, that they are accomplishing something. The amount of money you make is part of the satisfaction you get from work. Feeling that you have a chance to grow in the company you work for can be important. To be completely satisfied, you may need all of these feelings. When these needs aren't met, you probably feel dissatisfied and unhappy. That's when it's time to review your goals.

Your future depends on you. You'll have many challenges. If you try your best and don't reach a goal, you have not failed. Keep setting goals and keep going after them. That's how you climb the ladder of success in the world of work.

GLOSSARY

EXPLAINING NEW WORDS

application Printed form filled out by job-hunters that gives personal information to employers.
aptitude Natural talent or ability in a skill area.
career Job path you follow in the world of work.
characteristics Qualities or traits that make up a person.
cover letter Letter sent with a résumé or application to an employer.
employment agency Business that helps people find jobs for a fee.
entry-level job Job that requires little or no experience.
fringe benefits Benefits such as health insurance, sick leave, or vacation given to an employee in addition to salary or wages.
income Money earned by a worker.
interview Meeting between an applicant and employer to talk about a job.
on-the-job training Skill development while employee is working, usually under supervision.

personnel office Department of a company that hires workers.

résumé Short written summary of education, job skills, and work experience.

social security number Identifying number of workers who pay into the social security retirement system.

trade Field of skilled labor, such as carpenters, plumbers, or electricians.

unskilled Without job training or special abilities.

want ads Newspaper notices of job openings.

FOR FURTHER READING

Biegileisen, J.I. *Job Résumés*. New York: Perigee Books, Putman Publishing Group, 1991.

Bolles, Richard Nelson. *The New Quick Job Hunting Map*. Berkeley, CA: Ten Speed Press, 1990.

Boyd, Elza Dinwiddie. *How to Write a Résumé*. Stamford, CT: Longmeadow Press, 1991.

Half, Robert. *How to Get a Better Job in this Crazy World*. New York: Penguin Group, 1990.

Kaufman, Phyllis C., and Corrigan, Arnold. *No Nonsense Interviewing: How to Get the Job You Want*. Stamford, CT: Longmeadow Press, 1988.

Krannich, Ronald L., and Caryl Rae. *Discover the Right Job for You*. Woodbridge, VA: Impact Publications, 1991.

INDEX

A
application, job, 25
aptitude, 12

B
"being a good employee," 30
   six characteristics of, 30, 33–34
budget, 35, 36-37
   balancing of, 37
   necessities vs. luxuries, 37

C
career advancement, 7, 44
career goals, 42, 44
   long-range, 42
choices, 8

D
Dictionary of Occupational Titles, 41

H
high school, 8
   career center, 9, 42
   work experience program, 8
honors and awards, 19

I
interests, 13, 19
   and abilities, 10, 19

interview, 25, 26, 28, 29
   dress for, 28
   getting ready for, 28
   follow-up letter, 29

J
"job as business deal," 7
job satisfaction, 44
job search, 22–24

M
money (see budget)

O
Occupational Outlook Handbook, 42
Occupational Outlook Quarterly, 42
"on-the-job training," 8

P
personality traits, 9, 10, 13–14
physical characteristics, 9, 14

R
references (see résumé)
responsibilities of employees, 30, 33–34
   attendance, 33
   attitude, 34

following instructions, 33
loyalty, 33
responsibility, 33
willingness to work, 34
responsibilities of employer
  clean, safe place to work, 32
  fair treatment, 33
  fringe benefits, 33
  payment, 32
  training and supervision, 32
résumé, 18–19, 26
  and cover letter, 25
  education, 18
  example of, 20
  references, 19
  work experience, 18–19

S
skills, 7, 8
social security number, 16
"strengths and weaknesses," 9, 10, 14

T
time management, 38–40
  budget for, 40
training, 7

U
unskilled jobs, 7, 8

W
work experience, 8, 18–19

About the Author

Rhoda McFarland has taught all grades, kindergarten through twelfth. She is a certified alcoholism and drug abuse counselor having worked with troubled young people and their parents. She developed and implemented the first educational program in the California area for students making the transition from drug/alcohol treatment programs back into the regular school system. She was a Peace Corps Volunteer in Belize, Central America. Currently, she is the Life Skills Counselor at a high school in the Florida Keys.

Photo Credits
Cover photos: (top left and right) by Stuart Rabinowitz, (bottom left) by Dru Nadler, (bottom right) by Ned Gerard; pages 4, 23, 31, 43: Stuart Rabinowitz; pages 11, 27, 39: Ned Gerard; page 17: Dru Nadler; page 44: Chuck Peterson.

Design & Production: Blackbirch Graphics, Inc.